COMIC RELIEF

JULIA BROWN

(SERIES EDITOR: ROB ALCRAFT)

Heinemann
LIBRARY

First published in Great Britain by Heinemann Library

Halley Court, Jordan Hill, Oxford OX2 8EJ
a division of Reed Educational and Professional Publishing Ltd

OXFORD FLORENCE PRAGUE MADRID ATHENS
MELBOURNE AUCKLAND KUALA LUMPUR SINGAPORE TOKYO
IBADAN NAIROBI KAMPALA JOHANNESBURG GABORONE
PORTSMOUTH NH CHICAGO MEXICO CITY SAO PAULO

A 3% royalty on all copies of this book sold by Heinemann Library will be donated to Comic Relief, a registered charity, number 326568.

Produced by Plum Creative (01590 612970)
Printed in China

01 00 99 98 97
10 9 8 7 6 5 4 3 2 1

ISBN 0 431 02758 7

British Library Cataloguing in Publication Data
    Brown, Julia
    Comic Relief. - (Taking Action)
    1. Comic Relief - Juvenile literature
    I. Title
    361.7'632'0941

Comic Relief would like to thank the following for the generous help they have provided during production of this book:

Carisbrooke High School, Isle of Wight; CETA Services Ltd; Christian Aid; Heartsease High School, Norwich; Pete Grant; St. Martin-in-the-Fields High School, Stockwell, London; Tuffnells Parcels Express - especially their Same Day division; The Vineyard School, Richmond; Womankind Worldwide

Acnowledgements
The publishers would like to thank the following for permission to reproduce photographs:

Craig Barritt/Retna; George Bodnar; Bristol Evening Post; Ray Burmiston/Retna; Mauro Carraro/BBC; Derby Evening Telegraph; Hugo Dixon; Eastern Daily Press; Essex County Newspapers; Richard Graham; Peter Grant; Huddersfield Examiner; Beverley Jones; Peter Knab; Trevor Leighton; Ken Lennox; Live & Kicking Magazine © BBC Worldwide Limited 1997; Jason Lowe; Northampton Chronicle & Echo; Pacemaker Press; Plymouth Evening Herald; Chris Ridley/Radio Times; Bill Robinson; Jonathan Ruffle; Julia Simmons; Damian Walker; Wolverhampton Express & Star.

All photographs of The Spice Girls reproduced by kind permission of The Spice Girls. All rights reserved.

ANIMANIACS, characters, names and all related indicia are trademarks of Warner Bros. © 1997

Cover illustration by Scott Rhodes.

Every effort has been made to contact copyright holders of any material in this book. Any omissions will be rectified in subsequent printings if notice is given to the publisher.

Comic Relief Ltd is a subsidiary of Comic Relief, Registered Charity No. 326568.

All words in the text appearing in bold like **this** are explained in the Glossary.

CONTENTS

THE BIG PICTURE

Comic Relief started in 1985, with a television broadcast from a **refugee** camp in Sudan. The idea came from people in the charity world and the world of **media** and comedy. They wanted to use the media – especially television – to raise support for people facing the toughest challenges in Africa and the UK.

A BETTER CHANCE

Ever since it began, Comic Relief has tried to provide help for the people who need it most. It does this because it believes that everyone deserves a chance to achieve the brilliant things that they are capable of. Whatever problems people face – like **poverty**, **prejudice**, or being homeless – with the right help at the right time, it is possible to overcome them and move on.

One of the most important things that Comic Relief has learned is that working to solve problems can be a powerful and fun experience. It could be villagers in Ethiopia building a well, or young people in Brighton writing a newspaper about issues like drugs. But working together to achieve these small changes can make a real difference to people's lives.

When Comic Relief raises money, it wants the people who respond to have a lot of fun too. Every two years, Red Nose Day allows people to act out their wildest ideas – raising money, raising a laugh, and raising understanding about the problems people face and how they can be overcome.

◀ **Teacher Mr Garlinge gets well and truly splatted on Red Nose Day.**

▶ **Ruby Wax rolls around in the Red Nose readies.**

Since 1985, the public has raised over £130 million for Comic Relief.

MONEY WHERE IT'S NEEDED

In the UK, Comic Relief funds organizations that work with young people who are disabled, homeless, or having problems with drugs and alcohol, and organizations which improve the quality of life for people over 65.

◄ **Arthur Magill, Michelle Kenny and Jim Allen of PANDA (People Against Narcotics, Drugs and Alcohol) in Belfast. Comic Relief has supported their work by providing running costs and helping to set up an alcohol-free bar.**

▼ MONEY WHERE IT'S NEEDED

In Africa, Comic Relief funds local projects working with disabled people, pastoral people (who keep animals for their living), women, people who live in towns and cities, and people who are living through a conflict or war.

Here, Lenny Henry celebrates the first Red Nose Day in 1988 with children in Ethiopia.

5

The money has been donated to over 4000 projects in Africa and the UK.

PEOPLE LIKE YOU

People like you are really important to Comic Relief. Young people are the most dedicated Red Nose supporters. Over the years, they have come up with some outrageous ways of raising the cash (like racing their pet snails or taking Brussels sprouts for a walk).

Equally important are the young people who benefit from Comic Relief funds. A big chunk of the money raised on Red Nose Day is passed on to charities working with children or teenagers, who are often the most **vulnerable** members of a community.

Comic Relief also believes that young people can make a difference in the world. In its education work, Comic Relief tries to help young people to learn about some of the issues that concern them – like **poverty** in Africa, and homelessness in the UK. It produces video packs for use in schools, and runs competitions which encourage young people to express their ideas about the things they care about.

► **The *Going Live!* studio in 1993. Lenny Henry and Sarah Greene celebrate the fabulous fund-raising of Carisbrooke High School on the Isle of Wight.**

Over half the schools in the UK take part in Red Nose Day.

▶ Members of HAFAD (Hammersmith and Fulham Action for Disability) in London, which has received funds from Comic Relief. HAFAD helps disabled people to get the services they're entitled to.

SAINT BENEDICT SCHOOL
DUFFIELD ROAD
DERBY DE22 1JD

▲ Billy Connolly at Quelimane orphanage in Mozambique in 1989. During the long and fierce war in Mozambique, many children were separated from their parents. Comic Relief gave money to Save the Children, which was trying to reunite children with their families.

▶ Lenny gets tropical to advertise *Teacher Relief 1* – Comic Relief's education pack for 8–13 year olds about issues like poverty, disability and homelessness.

7

Comic Relief sends the Red Nose Newsletter to 33,000 schools twice each year.

BEHIND THE NOSE

Comic Relief has organized six Red Nose Days since 1985. Each time it's like throwing a huge party for the whole country. It takes months of planning and hard work – and then there's all the clearing up afterwards!

But when the party is over, Comic Relief's work carries on behind the scenes at its 'parent' organization called Charity Projects – the face behind the Nose. At the Charity Projects' office in central London, staff and experts make all the decisions about how the Red Nose money is spent. They also keep in touch with the projects that they fund and with all the Comic Relief supporters.

Lenny Henry with oodles of donated office supplies.

Staff at Charity Projects in 1995. (Who let Mr Bean get in on the act?)

Each year, around 250 companies donate everything from computers to paper clips to keep Comic Relief going.

Around 35 staff work at Charity Projects full-time. They do different jobs – from answering the phones to coming up with designs for the Red Nose. One thing that they all have to be good at is persuading people to do things for free. Comic Relief makes a promise to the public that, for every pound they raise, a pound is passed on to a charity in Africa or the UK. So Comic Relief relies on companies to keep the organization going by donating things like office equipment, printing and paper, and even tea and coffee, for free.

Press Manager Debra Deaville visits the Latin American Elderly Group in Islington, London. Comic Relief keeps in close touch with the projects it supports.

Robbie Coltrane is interviewed by Comic Relief fund-raiser Celia Perry at DASH (Drug Advice and Support in Hulme). The *celebrities* who support Comic Relief help out between Red Nose Days by talking to the *media*.

9

After Red Nose Day '95, there were over 12,000 enquiries from organizations seeking funding from Comic Relief.

COUNTDOWN TO RED NOSE DAY

JANUARY - JULY '96

Preparing for Red Nose Day takes well over a year – so it's a good thing the big event only happens every *two* years! Here's an inside look at key moments in the run-up to Red Nose Day '97. Comic Relief was determined to make this one BIGGER, **redder** and better than ever before!

January Approach Delia Smith to see whether she'll help out on Red Nose Day – it could be a delia-licious partnership!

February Lenny Henry agrees to make a film following the lives of young people living on the streets of London over the next year.

March Start to pick the nose! Favourites are a nose you can eat, one with wings, one which grows (like Pinocchio's!), and one with a built-in moustache. Difficult choice!

▶ Tony Robinson with the nose that got picked! It's shaggy, it's cute, and it's bound to tickle everyone who wears it.

▼ Delia comes up trumps! All proceeds from her Red Nose Recipe Booklet are donated to Comic Relief, and she records five 5-minute recipe programmes with *celebrities*, to broadcast during the run-up to Red Nose Day.

▲ Lenny interviews Mark Pearson during *Walk on By*.

▶ Ben & Jerry's becomes *Len & Jerry's*. 50p from every tub of *Fudge Behaving Badly* ice cream is donated to Comic Relief.

The new car nose was tested in a wind tunnel at speeds of 80 mph to check that it wouldn't fall off!

April T-shirt month. Think about putting the sponsorship form on a T-shirt. Also approach Warner Brothers to see whether any of their cartoon characters can be used. Fingers crossed!

May Mmmmm! It's time to test out flavours for a Comic Relief ice cream produced by Ben & Jerry's, plus possible sweets to put inside the new Red Nose.

June Start making the most ambitious Comic Relief film ever – a team of football-mad celebrities visits Africa, to play against local teams and find out about Comic Relief projects along the way.

July All the Red Nose Day ideas and products are really beginning to take shape. The car nose leaves the front bumper, sticks on to the windscreen and will be sold by Texaco. Umbro will make red footballs for people to do sponsored 'keepy uppy'; The Body Shop will create a Kissing Kit so people can keep a 'snog log' of sponsored smackeroos!

Sketches for the 'sponsorship form on a T-shirt' idea, plus Simon (of 'Trevor and Simon' fame) demonstrates the final version featuring *Animaniacs* characters Yakko, Wakko, Dot, Pinky and the Brain.

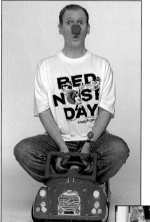

Frank Skinner and David Baddiel learn new dribbling skills during filming for *Balls to Africa – Sporting Noses on Tour*.

Celebrity demonstrations of the Red Nose products: singer Louise puckering up with The Body Shop Kissing Kit, Richard Wilson with the windscreen car nose, and David Seaman with the 'keepy uppy' football.

11

Comic Relief produced over a million brochures and leaflets to tell the world about plans for the big day.

COUNTDOWN CONTINUES

AUGUST '96 - MARCH '97

August The big theme for the day is decided – *Small Change, Big Difference*. The plan is to encourage everyone to turn out their pockets, dive down their sofas, raid their piggy banks, and spend all their pennies on Comic Relief.

September Start to write *Red Mag* – the Comic Relief fund-raising magazine which will tell the great British public how they can get involved.

October Twenty extra Red Nose Day staff come on-board to help prepare for the big day. Work begins on Red News Day, a package of materials to help schools and youth groups get their fund-raising events into the local media.

November Polygram agree to produce 800,000 almost life-size posters of Mr Bean for people to advertise their event. The 'extra bits' in the nose are finalized – a Chupa Chups red tongue-painting lolly, plus a 'nosebag' for collecting small change.

SMALL CHANG
BIG
DIFFERENC
**RED NOSE DA
MARCH 14TH '9**

The logo for Red Nose Day '97. Gary Olsen puts it into action.

Over half a million *Red Mags* are sent out. It's a record!

Hitting the headlines with Red News Day. Over 4000 schools got involved, persuading their local media to turn them into stars for the day.

In Africa, 3p buys a pen for a child in Senegal learning to read and write.

December Julie Walters agrees to visit Ethiopia to make a film about children living on the street. A great end to the year.

1997

January The new year starts with the best news ever – the Spice Girls have agreed to donate proceeds from their next single – *Who Do You Think You Are?* – to Comic Relief. Grrrrl Power!

February Everyone is getting very nervous now, with only one month to go. Staff at the BBC are hard at work, editing all the sketches and planning all the comedy and serious bits for the night of TV. There is so much good stuff, they're worried about fitting it all in to the programme.

March It's nearly here! 750,000 Red Noses have already been sold, thousands of people are standing-by across the country to do their fund-raising events, the **celebrities** are rehearsing the show for the big night … everyone is very *very* nervous, and *ridiculously* excited! Will the public respond?

▶ **Things start hotting up outside BBC Television Centre during filming for a crowd scene to be shown on the big night.**

◀ **Ainsley Harriott with all the nosey bits.**

▲ **Julie Walters gets to nose a group of children during filming of her documentary about street children in Addis Ababa, Ethiopia.**

◀ **The Spice Girls meet the Sugar Lumps (Dawn French, Jennifer Saunders, Kathy Burke and Llewella Gideon). Will the *real* Spice Girls please stand up?**

▼ **Jimmy Hill gets blasted in a sketch for the Night of Comic Relief TV.**

In the UK, £12 provides a bed for the night for a homeless young person.

THE BIG DAY
BLOW BY BLOW

We nose who you are! The shaggy nose becomes the favourite hot fashion item in schools across the UK.

March 14th 1997 dawns bright and sunny. Across the country, thousands of people wake up with the knowledge that this is going to be a very funny Friday indeed. Meanwhile, in London, the Red Nose Day team are quaking in their boots. Will this be the stonking success they have all been working for?

FUNNY BUSINESS

In schools, offices, factories and high streets, people begin to act *extremely* strangely. A rash of red noses breaks out, teachers let their hair down, thousands of mini-Spice Girls strut their stuff, baths overflow with yuk and banks begin to burst at the seams with bucket-loads of pennies.

Teachers at Allen Edwards Primary School in Stockwell, London, show their true colours.

Steve Phillips of Bristol City football team isn't quite sure what's hit him! Body Shop assistants Susie McLoughlin and Slaudia Spoto test out their kissing kits in Broadmead High Street.

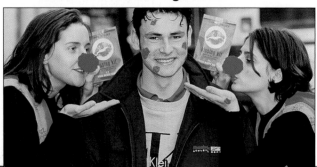

Over 10,000 people told Comic Relief that they were planning fund-raising events.

Spice Girl wannabes Alison Fletcher, Rebecca Fieldhouse, Natalie Hughes, Samantha Cotterill and Stephanie Fellows shake their stuff in Wolverhampton on Red Nose Day. Meanwhile, Dawn French, Jennifer Saunders, Kathy Burke and Llewella Gideon (also known as The Sugar Lumps) get in on the act in their bedroom, during filming for the Spice Girls' video.

Runners warm-up at the start of a Fun Run in the City of London.

Eastenders star Paul Nicholls relaxes in a nice bath ... thank goodness he was caught with his clothes on!

Danny Early and Damian Boreham are no cowardy-custards! They cycled from Halstead to Braintree wearing custard-filled wellies in aid of Comic Relief.

IN SCHOOLS ...

Everyone gets to have fun, wear red, go stupid and get wild!

IN HIGH STREETS ...

Strangers kiss each other, the Spice Girls shake buckets and people get on their bikes wearing custard-filled wellies!

IN BATHS ...

People get dunked, splunked, gunked ... and very, very sticky.

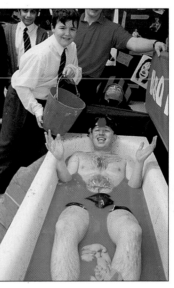

Mark Brooke of Salendine Nook High School, Huddersfield, takes great pleasure in topping up teacher Lyn Davies's bath – with spaghetti and baked beans.

15

Children who are 10 in 1998 will have experienced Red Nose Days ever since they were born!

THE BIG NIGHT BLOW BY BLOW

ON WITH THE SHOW

By six in the evening, BBC Television Centre in West London is throbbing with anticipation. Crowds of people are descending to join the studio audience, or just to watch the arrival of Boyzone and the Spice Girls. The Comic Relief staff are marching around like a small red army, making sure that everything goes to plan. The **celebrities** are safely in their dressing rooms, running over their lines. And across the country, people are settling-in for one of the best telly nights of the year.

▲ The studio audience are flushed with anticipation!

◄ Theophilus P. Wildebeest has his wicked way with Delia Smith. She'll never be the same again!

◄ Paul Bradley (Nigel in *Eastenders*) shows what he's really made of for a special edition of *Gladiators*.

▶ Behind the scenes, Comic Relief staff take phone calls from the public who want more information about what's happening on screen.

During one five-minute period, there were around 66,000 telephone calls on the donation line.

◀ Children in Addis Ababa, Ethiopia, give the thumbs up. Julie Walters' film about street children in Addis gives a real boost to donations.

▶ Jonathan Ross and Griff Rhys Jones beg the public to donate £100,000 so that they can be kissed by the Spice Girls. It works, much to their delight. Here Geri gets her man!

By 9pm, the BT staff taking donations on the telephone line are going into overdrive. The total amount raised has reached £4.6 million. The Comic Relief staff are stunned into silence. No one can quite believe that the public have done it – again!

▲ Smashey and Nicey (Harry Enfield and Paul Whitehouse) do their bit for 'charidy'.

▲ The action moves from Television Centre to the live comedy show at the Shepherd's Bush Empire.

▶ The Spice Girls and the Sugar Lumps live on stage.

By the end of the night, the public had donated £11.68 million to Comic Relief, breaking all records.

SUPPORTING WOMEN IN GHANA

◀ **Ndego Asimiga with her grandchildren. Loans from BEWDA have helped Ndego sell products in the local market, and buy food, education and medicine for her family.**

Comic Relief passes on money to many projects which work with women in Africa, because it knows they suffer some of the greatest hardships and have the heaviest responsibilities. And we know that, when women are poor, their children suffer too.

BEWDA stands for Bawku East Women's Development Agency. It's a voluntary organization helping women in 17 villages in northern Ghana in West Africa. There are high rates of **malnutrition** here, and many people (especially women) haven't had the chance to learn to read and write.

In Ghana, as in other parts of Africa, land and property are mainly controlled by men. This means that women find it difficult to be **independent**, to run their own businesses, or to get loans from banks and money-lenders. Often, they aren't able to set up the small businesses that would help them out of **poverty**.

WORKING TOGETHER

BEWDA has tried to help local women by setting up a kind of 'people's bank'. Groups of 25 women join together to form a 'borrower circle'. Each woman in the circle applies to the rest of the group for a loan. The whole circle then applies to BEWDA for a group loan. The money is used to buy tools, supplies and equipment so women can run small businesses like making butter, or growing vegetables for selling in the local market. Despite the poverty of many of the women involved, nearly all the loans get paid back. The women know that if they miss a payment, they will be letting down everyone in the group.

After Red Nose Day, Comic Relief does research to ensure that money goes where it's needed most.

➤ Members of BEWDA in Nyorigu village with David Essex, Ainsley Harriott, and John Leslie during the making of a Comic Relief film. Loans from BEWDA help the women to buy *sorghum*, which they mix with malt and sell to brewers in the local town to make beer.

▲ Girls from Nyorigu village. As in many parts of Africa, girls have to help out in the home and with the younger children from an early age. Organizations like BEWDA will help girls like these have a brighter future.

▲ This is Mustapha Dauda. He is 13. He had to leave school recently because his father couldn't pay his fees (most schools in Africa aren't free). With help from BEWDA, more families can afford to send their children to school.

19

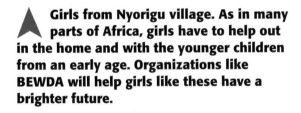

Between 1995 and 1997, Comic Relief gave £2,653,598 to 45 projects working with women across Africa.

EDUCATION IN THE NUBA MOUNTAINS

The Nuba mountain region in the centre of Sudan is home to the Nuba people – a group of tribes which makes up one of Africa's oldest societies. For 13 years, Sudan has been in a state of **civil war**, and the Nuba people have suffered terribly. Villages have been burnt, and people have been executed or forced to move from their homes. Now the region is more or less cut off from the outside world and people are suffering from years of fighting and neglect.

FUNDS FOR SCHOOLING

In early 1996, a group of organizations got together to help the Nuba people to set up farming, health and education projects. Comic Relief has been funding the education programme, which is run by Christian Aid. Since 1987, there had been no proper education system in the region because of the fighting, but despite this, local volunteers kept on working with out-of-date textbooks to give Nuba children basic schooling.

Now Christian Aid is helping children to catch up properly on their education. Eighty-seven schools have been rebuilt, and basic equipment like pens, blackboards and textbooks is getting through. Teachers are also receiving proper training, including how to look after children who have been badly affected by the war. This is just one of many projects funded by Comic Relief to help people in Africa affected by conflict or war.

► **Children of Ragifay village. The children in the picture have lived in a state of war all their lives.**

Staff make regular trips to Africa to visit projects funded by Comic Relief.

◀ A group of young Nuba men. Since the war started, the choices for young men are very few – they can either join the rebels who are fighting the government, or leave the region completely and face *discrimination* in other parts of the country.

◀ Children outside Ragifay church singing a song that asks for freedom from the war.

▶ A young boy waiting for a relief plane to arrive gazes into the sky. Since the war started, it has been very difficult to get supplies to the Nuba region. Equipment for the education programme funded by Comic Relief has had to be flown in by plane bit by bit.

Between 1995 – 1997, Comic Relief gave £2,881,827 to projects working with people affected by war in Africa.

HOUSING IN HULL

Comic Relief has found that young people, and people over 65, face some of the hardest circumstances in the UK. It also knows that they have some brilliant projects to help themselves.

TAKING ACTION

In 1985, a group of young people in Hull who were facing unemployment and homelessness decided to take matters into their own hands. They called themselves Giroscope and scraped together enough money to buy a run-down house. They **renovated** it, and taught themselves building skills as they went along.

When the first house was ready, they realized that the idea couldn't stop there. Too many people faced similar problems. So they kept going, passing on skills and renovating properties, and now they have helped to provide 17 houses and 4 flats, which are home to 45 young adults and 18 children.

Giroscope isn't just a housing organization. It gives people the chance to learn useful skills, organizes social events, and has helped to start a corner shop. All this has brought people together in a poor part of Hull which has high unemployment.

Giroscope is now working on a site which will house a group of young people with learning disabilities who want to be **independent** and have their own home. Old garages behind the house will contain workshops for small businesses – giving even more young people a better chance to get on with their lives.

▼ **Ian and his daughter Eleanor leaving their house. Giroscope housed Ian and his family in 1994. 'Moving in was one of the best days of my life.' Now Ian works with Giroscope as a builder.**

Comic Relief has given Giroscope £37,000 to help homeless young people since 1988.

Martin, Rob, Jenny and Ian of Giroscope take a break from renovating a house for young people with learning disabilities. Strangely, they like to wear red noses and show off their tools when they're relaxing!

Inside the People's Trading Company corner shop, which Giroscope helped to set up.

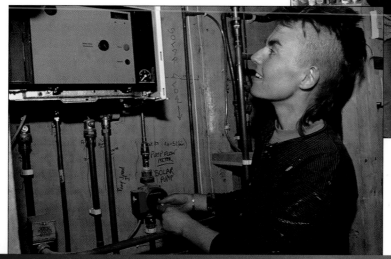

Jenny plumbing in a *solar* water heater. Giroscope try to make sure their buildings harm the *environment* as little as possible.

23

Between 1995 and 1997, Comic Relief gave £2,102,770 to projects working with homeless people in the UK.

DRAMA IN DYFED

Imagine going to the theatre to see *Hamlet* by William Shakespeare. Hamlet spends most of the play standing around, wondering what to do, while people around him do dreadful deeds! Then imagine you stand up and tell Hamlet who's doing what, and how he can solve it all.

That's almost what Theatr Fforwm Cymru (Forum Theatre Wales) lets young people do.

JOINING IN

Working with puppets or live performers, the company performs a play dealing with an issue that's important to young people. Things like drugs, alcohol, **AIDS** or bullying. Then the performers stop the action and encourage the audience to join in and change what happens. It's a great way of giving young people a chance to solve problems they face in their lives.

Gill Dowsett and Anna Gifford set up Theatr Fforwm in 1994. Now they have trained a group of young volunteers to do the performances.

These volunteers get **GNVQ** qualifications along the way. In 1995, their shows were seen by 6000 young people in schools and youth clubs in rural parts of Wales. This is just one of the many projects funded by Comic Relief to help young people deal with the tough challenges of drugs and alcohol.

A Theatr Fforwm puppet show in progress at Neyland Infants School.

All the projects funded by Comic Relief send in a report each year about their work.

▼ Volunteer youth workers at Theatr Fforwm showing off the puppets they work with. These puppets are from a show about bullying. Using puppets is a good way to show young children how to cope with difficult situations.

▼ Children of Mrs Griffith's class get a chance to handle the puppets and talk to the youth workers after the show.

▲ Bradley and Hannah, youth workers with Theatr Fforwm, have benefited from working with the company. 'I used to keep things to myself a lot and it taught me that I should speak out,' says Bradley. 'I'd been signing on for a year and I'd lost all confidence in myself. I needed something like this to feel good about myself,' says Hannah.

Between 1995 and 1997, Comic Relief gave £1,270,921 to young people with drug and alcohol problems.

VISION FOR THE FUTURE

Since the first broadcast from a **refugee** camp in Sudan in 1985, Comic Relief has come a long way. Millions of people have been involved in Red Nose Days, and many thousands of people have benefited from the money raised.

But what about the future? What new and exciting things can Comic Relief dream up to inspire people and raise money for the causes it supports? There are still millions of people in Africa and the UK whose lives could be improved with the right kind of help.

Wouldn't it be great to look into the future and find out what Comic Relief will be doing in the year 2000 and beyond? Here are some ideas from young people … why not write to Comic Relief at the address on page 30 with your own ideas for a Red Nose future?

➤ **'Jumping Red Noses' by Christine Griever, St Martin-in-the-Fields High School, London.**

A DREAM OF THE FUTURE

Smiling faces, no war places,
All the nations are united,
No poverty, no illnesses,
No need for stonking businesses,
A world free of war and crime
No need for help at charity time.
We've made the money, worn the nose,
To live in a world where anything goes
A time of happiness, freedom and fun
But this new life has just begun
We can live in peace together
And hope there's a world that lasts forever.

Morwenna Trevan, 15, and Louise Millar, 14, Carisbrooke High School, Isle of Wight

'What Comic Relief is doing will have an impact on all our lives, no matter who we are.' Toyin Kasali, St Martin-in-the-Fields High School, London.

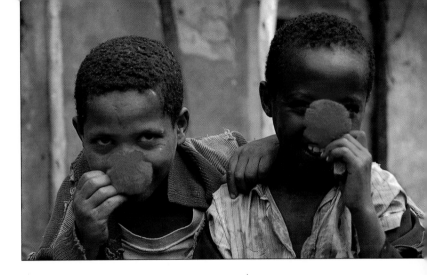

A street in London. A project worker from Cranstoun Projects Safe Outreach Team talks to a young man who's about to go into a nightclub about the side-effects of drugs and alcohol. This kind of work has a long-term impact, helping people to protect themselves from future problems with alcohol and drugs.

RED NOSE DAY IDEAS

- Plumbers go round to people's houses and turn a special switch to make their water turn red for the day.
- Get all the football teams in Division 1, 2 and 3 to play a match against each other at the same time. The ball can be a giant Red Nose-shaped football!
- Paint a town red for a day.

Francesca Buchanan, 10, Patrick Langley, 10, Melanie Hall, 11, The Vineyard School, Richmond

RED NOSE ZONE

Our idea is a Theme Park with Red Nose Rides. We would sell things related to Red Noses. One of our ideas is a 'Red Nose Dome' – it's a ball which people are strapped inside and the ball moves around. We would have a drinks machine called 'Runny Nose' which is a nose and you press a button and drink comes out of the nostrils. We would have a Red Nose Roller Coaster, a train in the shape of a long Red Nose which shows everyone the attractions and a 'Red Nose Splash' ride which goes round and into the water. You could also buy a 'Red Nose Mac'.

Rachel, Hannah, Zoe and Kerri, Heartsease High School, Norwich

Admarsu and Zeriyhun, two friends who live on the streets of Addis Ababa, Ethiopia. The boys make a living by picking up grains or coffee beans that have dropped onto the ground at local markets, and selling them. They regularly use a street children's shelter run by the Irish charity, GOAL, which has received support from Comic Relief. Their dreams of the future include getting an education, finding a decent job, and eventually being able to have a home of their own. With luck and the right support, their dreams could come true. But surely the best future would be one where children like these didn't have to end up living on the streets?

'Eventually, the people in Africa won't need our help any more – that's what Comic Relief is about'. Paul Prouse, Carisbrooke High School, Isle of Wight.

OVER TO YOU!

It's up to *you* to keep Comic Relief alive and kicking. Here are some things you can do any time to support Comic Relief.

Dream on… Comic Relief would love to hear your ideas: the people and events you would like to see on TV on Red Nose Day; how the charity can raise loads and loads of lovely money; or how it can help young people to find out about issues like **poverty** and homelessness.

Have fun… What do you love doing? What makes you laugh? Whatever gives you a kick, why not do it for Comic Relief? Next time you feel like holding a custard pie fight or watching your favourite video, why not turn it into a fund-raising event? You can have your own Red Nose Day any day, and donate the proceeds to Comic Relief.

Get Red Nosey… Find out what your friends and family would like to do to raise money on Red Nose Day, and help to get it organized. Comic Relief would love to hear of your activities, so don't forget to send us your photos or videos.

And finally… GET SERIOUS!
What do you think and feel about the lives of the people Comic Relief exists to help? Whether it's disabled people in the UK or people living through a war in Africa, find out about the serious problems facing people and how they can be overcome. Write to Comic Relief with your questions and ideas, or organize an event at your school. Over the page you will find our address and some other organizations which can help.

Around 20,000 copies of Comic Relief's education packs are now in schools around the UK.

▼ **Boyzone get carried away… giving a big 'THANK YOU' to all the young people who have helped Comic Relief over the years.**

▼ **Angus Deayton congratulates young people from Bollo Brook Youth Centre, who produced a brilliant cartoon about the effects of drugs for Comic Relief's *Video Relief* competition in 1995. Comic Relief runs regular competitions with BBC1's *Live & Kicking*. Keep your eyes peeled for the next one.**

▲ **Why not join the Barmy Army of Red Nose Supporters? Claire Szoludko and Julie Holmes of Bective Middle School in Northampton did!**

THANK Y●U, THANK Y●U, THANK Y●U to all the brilliant schools that support Comic Relief.

FURTHER INFORMATION

COMIC RELIEF – SERIOUS COMMITMENT

If you want to find out more about Comic Relief's work and how you can get serious about important issues, drop us a line. Or ask your teacher to get hold of a Comic Relief education pack for the classroom. Write to:

**The Education Department, Comic Relief,
74 New Oxford Street, London, WC1A 1EF**

Below are the names and addresses of other organizations that can give you information about some of the serious issues that Comic Relief works on. Be clear about what you want when you write to them, and save them money by sending a stamped, self-addressed envelope.

For information on serious issues in Africa:

ActionAid
Chataway House
Leach Road
Chard
Somerset TA20 IFA

Christian Aid
35-41 Lower Marsh
London SE1 7RL

Oxfam
274 Banbury Road
Oxford OX2 7DZ

Save the Children
Mary Datchelor House
17 Grove Lane
London SE5 8RD

For information about Development Education Centres in your local area, write to:

The Development Education Association
29-31 Cowper Street
London EC2A 4AP

For information on serious issues in the UK:

Disability
RADAR
12 City Forum
250 City Road
London EC1V 8AF

Homelessness
Shelter
88 Old Street
London ECIV 9HO

Drugs and alcohol
TACADE
1 Hulme Place
The Crescent
Manchester M5 4QA

Older people
Age Concern
Astral House
1268 London Road
London SW16 4ER

Get nosey!

GLOSSARY

AIDS this stands for Auto Immune Deficiency Syndrome, a condition which makes people less able to fight off ordinary illnesses or get better from them

celebrities famous people, often actors or pop stars

civil war a war between different groups of people living in the same country

discrimination picking on people and treating them differently from others, often for unfair reasons

environment the surroundings in which humans, animals and other living creatures live, like seas, rivers, forests, air, or buildings in towns and cities

GNVQ qualifications which people take, usually between the ages of 16 and 19. They are the initials for General National Vocational Qualification. They help people prepare for jobs in business and industry

independent not depending on anyone or anything else for your livelihood

media newspapers, magazines, radio, television, satellite and other ways of communicating with a large number of people

malnutrition not having enough of the strength and energy that we get from eating enough proper food

poverty people living in poverty are often poor, with little money to buy things. But it can also mean having no access to education, healthcare, shelter, safety, or food and drink

prejudice making up your mind about something or someone before knowing the facts

refugee a person who has to leave their home or country because of a war or another situation that threatens their safety or their lives

renovate to improve something so that it is in a better condition

solar powered by the sun

sorghum a type of grain which is grown in some countries

vulnerable unprotected, and at risk of being harmed

▼ **Joanna Lumley gets to grips with her script while filming for Comic Relief in Eritrea.**

INDEX